Secret Endorsements

"In the tradition of *The Christmas Box*, *Life's Little Instruction Book*, and *Everything I Know I Learned in Kindergarten*, *The 12 Best Secrets of Christmas* strikes a graceful, delightful, and literate universal chord."

> – **Robert S. Ray** (Film, Television and Literary Scholar)

"Like *The Homecoming: A Christmas Story*, this book harkens back to a simpler time...with sweet holiday messages for a complicated world. Herbie J Pilato lived those messages...and now shares them with the rest of us."

> – **Mary McDonough** (Actor/Author, *Christmas on Honeysuckle Lane/ Lessons from the Mountain: What I Learned from Erin Walton*)

"With this book, Herbie J has given us a gift of words that we can celebrate each and every day."

> – **David Selby** (Actor, *Dark Shadows*, *Social Network*, *Falcon Crest*/Author, *Promises of Love*)

"In a time when society is losing its wonder of the holidays, a book like this comes along to remind us how important Christmas traditions can be for everyone, everywhere. The empowering life lessons presented here remind us to embrace how every nuance of Christmas can add up to meaningful, magical moments to last a lifetime."

> – **Eileen Grubba** (Actor, *This is Us*, *New Amsterdam*)

"Herbie J Pilato's early Christmas memories leap out of his heart and into our souls with wondrous lessons of life and light, each representing defining childhood moments. With the purest of prose, it's all documented with love, which Herbie J shares in abundance with every single word in this magnificent book."

– **Caryn Richman** (Actor, *The New Gidget*, *The Bradys*)

"Herbie J has a flair for making anything vintage feel contemporary. With *The 12 Best Secrets of Christmas*, he takes us on an almost visceral journey...a journey worth taking and reading."

– **Louis Herthum** (Actor, *Murder, She Wrote*, *Westworld*, *Longmire*)

"Herbie J Pilato's *The 12 Best Secrets of Christmas* is a charming collection of deeply personal, insightful memories of Christmas celebrated with his warm and loving extended family in Rochester, N.Y. These gem-like stories glitter with poignant messages of faith, hope, love, gratitude and, of course, holiday cheer."

– **Kathryn Leigh Scott** (Actor/Author/Book Publisher)

"Herbie J Pilato captures the universal spirit of Christmas, the time of the year that spreads joy and good feelings, brings families together, delights children with expectation, and warms the hearts of people everywhere."

– **Richard Michaels** (Director/Producer, *Bewitched*/
Script Supervisor, *Leave it to Beaver*)

"Such a warm, relatable story. Well done."

    – **Kathy Coleman** (Actor, *Land of the Lost*/Author, *Run, Holly Run*)

"I didn't realize how much I have in common with Herbie J Pilato until I read his *12 Best Secrets of Christmas*. Warm and fuzzy, sweet and intelligent, and full of humor, this masterpiece proves that people of all cultures have a common unifying trait, thread and bond of love."

    – **Irene Tsu** (Actor, *Star Trek, Wonder Woman*/Author, *A Water Color Dream: The Many Lives of Irene Tsu)*

"The generous way that Herbie J Pilato invites the reader to journey into a place of happiness is a gift in these times of uncertainty and challenge. His *12 Best Secrets of Christmas* reminds us that we each possess the blessing and the miracle of Christmas within us, always."

    – **Thomas Warfield** (Performing Artist/Founder, PeaceArt International/Director of Dance, Rochester Institute of Technology)

"*The 12 Best Secrets of Christmas* should be made known to the world."

    – **Rose Colombo** (Radio Host/Author, *Oops, What's the Name of My Lipstick!)*

"With *The 12 Best Secrets of Christmas*, Herbie J Pilato captures what we all may now cherish forever."

    – **Mickey O'Brien** (Medical Social Worker, Pilot and Stonemason, Ireland)

"In this sensitive book of untold treasures, Herbie J Pilato relays the charming recollections of his youth at Christmas, forging chapters that nurture the soul."

– **Barbara Messerle Devitt** (English Literature Teacher/Junior Statesman Advisor/BTSA Mentor - State of CA, Servite High School)

The 12 Best Secrets of Christmas reminds me of growing up in the working-class northeast side of Pennsylvania. We had our own set of Christmas traditions so very similar to Herbie J's and reading his eloquent Christmas memories made me tear up...in a good way. This book is a blessing to behold."

– **Vince Staskel** (Inclusion Advocate/Promoter for Performers-with-Disabilities)

"As children (from an earlier generation), we many times visited Herbie J Pilato's house at the corner of Erie and Warehouse Streets in Rochester, New York. His reminiscences in this book are spot on about the warmth and love that were evident in this simple Italian family household. Simple only in wealth, but there was richness beyond measure in the life values that were instilled in everyone that came in contact with this unique home. It's wonderful to spend some time with Herbie J and his relatives again, and it will be wonderful for those who have never met the family to do so through this beautiful book."

– **Rene Piacentini** (Rochester Historian) and Anne Piacentini Lawrence (Actor, *The Daily Show*)

The 12 Best Secrets of Christmas

A Treasure House of December Memories Revealed

HERBIE J PILATO

ARCHWAY
PUBLISHING

Archway Publishing books may be ordered through booksellers or by contacting:

Archway Publishing
1663 Liberty Drive
Bloomington, IN 47403
www.archwaypublishing.com
844-669-3957

Because of the dynamic nature of the Internet, any web addresses or links contained in this book may have changed since publication and may no longer be valid. The views expressed in this work are solely those of the author and do not necessarily reflect the views of the publisher, and the publisher hereby disclaims any responsibility for them.

Any people depicted in stock imagery provided by Getty Images are models, and such images are being used for illustrative purposes only.
Certain stock imagery © Getty Images.

Original book cover art by Carole Munshi.
Cover design by Bob Barnett, Dan Holm, and Terry DiOrio.

ISBN: 978-1-6657-1617-8 (sc)
ISBN: 978-1-6657-1618-5 (hc)
ISBN: 978-1-6657-1616-1 (e)

Library of Congress Control Number: 2021924863

Print information available on the last page.

Archway Publishing rev. date: 08/08/2022

Contents

Dedicated to Love, however it may be expressed and experienced by anyone of any culture, heritage, creed, political party, gender, sexual orientation, or religious or spiritual belief.

Foreword
by Dean Butler

I first met Herbie J Pilato a decade ago at an event in Burbank, CA. He invited me to join my friend, Caryn Richman, in a panel discussion he was moderating about classic television shows. Caryn and I co-starred on *The New Gidget* in the mid-1980s, and I've always enjoyed any opportunity to reflect on those days with her. We played Gidget and Moondoggie—it was silly good fun; "pink fluff," as our director, Roger Duchowny, often described it. As we reminisced, Caryn and I could see that Herbie J appreciated our pink fluff. Years later he was genuinely touched by cast reflections of the sweet sentimentality and goodness of Michael Landon's *Little House on the Prairie*. He had a fondness for both series, their places in television history, and how they influenced his life. Herbie J gets TV and loves its impact on audiences.

Herbie J has other loves too. His warm reverence for Christmas is genuinely present in *The 12 Best Secrets of Christmas: A Treasure House of December Memories Revealed*. Here, he shares a dozen traditions from his youth in Rochester, New York that have most deeply impacted his life from then to now. Herbie J's Christmas memories, with their connections to family, are deeply ingrained in the essential fabric of Western culture. As I read this book, I was struck by how similar his Christmas "secrets" are to mine, and I bet yours, too.

Regardless of our different religious traditions (Herbie J is a devout Roman Catholic while I was raised in a largely agnostic family) the holiday season, from Thanksgiving through New Year's, is a time that deeply touches the lives of our families. I get great comfort knowing that two different families share a similar joy at Christmas. Multiply that by millions of families and you have a season of joy all over the world.

Insights on how to make the season merry are what Herbie J writes about in this book. His "secrets" are in the music, the snow, in silver paper, holiday cards, a well-set table, and more. It's how all these things make us feel that's important. For me, the twinkling wonder of a beautiful tree, the holly and pinecones that adorn a wreath on the door, a crackling fire, and the smell of holiday spices in the kitchen are the perfect backdrop for the holiday entertainment that Herbie J and I both love. *Rudolph the Red-Nosed Reindeer, A Charlie Brown Christmas,* and *It's a Wonderful Life* are must-see holiday viewing. If we all got together, we could fill pages with entertainment that make our holidays merry. Regardless of what we love about the holidays, Herbie J understands that we are joined together by the feelings our favorite things elicit in us, and we are better for them.

Now in the 21st century, as our cultural touchstones expand, it has never been more important for us to find and celebrate gratitude during the holidays.

With this book, Herbie J Pilato shares his *12 Best Secrets of Christmas* and encourages each of us to embrace, enjoy, and discover our own with those we love.

Introduction
by Jerry Houser

I was fortunate enough to voice the holiday television promos for CBS for over 20 years. During that time, the most anticipated show every year was *Rudolph the Red-Nosed Reindeer*. Herbie J Pilato's loving recollection of that special alone makes this book a wonderful Christmas read.

With *The 12 Best Secrets of Christmas*, Herbie J relays in words what makes Christmas so very special to so many. I'd forgotten many of the wonderful things that Herbie J so eloquently remembers and clarifies here. How wonderful to be lost in his unique style of expression that allows the reader to enjoy the magic of Christmas snow, only to be reminded of things like snow's "more solid, cinnamon-colored cousin… the sand on the beach."

Herbie J so beautifully captures the unique moments of innocence and delight that make childhood precious and filled with wide-eyed wonder. He speaks from the heart, and remembers, for one, the comfort and joy of his mother receiving a Christmas card that made him think to appreciate those who deliver them. "Although they may not be doctors," Herbie J recalls, "…the postal carriers who bear their printed gifts still fix hearts each time they deliver just the right piece of mail. Sure, these are also the same people who bring us bills, but at least they don't collect them."

Those are the kinds of gems you will find, and assuredly embrace, within these pages.

Preface

I was raised within a large Catholic Italian-American family in the 1960s and 1970s. My father never made much money, but we didn't have many bills. For a good portion of my childhood, we lived in the home of my mother's family, located on Erie Street, a historic district of Rochester near the Erie Canal.

Our house was a modest, humble duplex made of solid red brick, stone, and lots of love. I lived on one side with my parents, Herbert Pompeii Pilato and Frances Turri Pilato, my older sibling Pamela Rose, and our Aunt Mary, the eldest of my mother's sisters. "Next door," as we used to call it, lived my Aunt Elva Turri Easton, one of my mom's other siblings, her husband Carl, and their daughter, my cousin Evie, who was like a sister to Pam and me.

Constructed in the 1880s, our house was initially built as the servants' quarters to a mansion that once stood beside it, while the structure in between our residence and the mansion had first been used as a stable for horses. As it happened, this sturdy estate was situated across the street from the Haloid Company—the original global office of the

Xerox Corporation. This renowned business was positioned in the shadow of another—the international home office of the Eastman Kodak Company. And all of that was just two blocks from Brown Square Park, and one block shy of where now stands the famed Frontier Field.

At one point, Kodak had purchased most of the residential small business properties in our neighborhood with the intent to transform the entire area into parking facilities for their employees. Most every house and business were demolished, except for our house, which was protected by the Landmark Society – and maybe a few angels. Either way, it was clearly built to last.

As part of its original design, our house had no front porch or overlapping roof, both of which my maternal grandfather added later. Initially, the house was situated at the corner of Erie Street and Warehouse Street, which at one point led to Platt Street to the east, and Brown Street to the west. Warehouse Street was named so because it was lined with various factories, which had loading docks, where I used to put on plays and shows with the neighborhood kids. It was just like in those classic Andy Hardy movies from the 1930s and '40s starring Mickey Rooney and Judy Garland.

In 1970, the state, the county, and the city decided to build an expressway twenty yards from our side windows, atop a new hill made of imported mounds of soil and cement. As a result, more residences and factories crumbled, and that's when Warehouse Street became our driveway.

It was an untraditional place to live for a family that was born into "tradition." It was also a good life, even though I had nothing of what this world calls "secure." But we were clean and healthy, the house was spotless, we ate well, never went hungry, and loved God. We attended church every Sunday morning and enjoyed pasta every Sunday afternoon, and Tuesday and Thursday night. For dinner on Monday and Wednesday, my mother served her savory homemade chicken or lentil soup. Come Friday night, we went out to eat.

Both of my parents hailed from large families, which extended our immediate brood to include numerous aunts, uncles, and cousins. As a result, there was a party of some sort almost every night at our house, which was considered "the house"—the hub of the family. Every relative and beyond; neighbors and friends were also frequent visitors to this grand central station where it all happened.

The company we kept included siblings Rene Piacentini and Anne Piacentini Lawrence, whose Uncle Val was married to one of my mother's sisters, Amelia. As Anne once said, that made her and her brother my "cousins-in-law."

The Piacentini siblings first visited Erie Street in their tween years, when Palma Turri, my mother's mom, known as Nonna, was still alive. As Rene once told me, "Palma was tiny in stature, but a giant in the household and neighborhood."

In that household was a set of encyclopedias that Rene utilized to their fullest extent in his young academic life. "I credit the nights, studying, on Erie Street, for doing well in school," he told me another time.

In short, Erie Street was where everyone wanted to be, no matter how much or how little money anyone had. Many a day my mom even welcomed a homeless soul or two into the house for a meal. That's the way we did it. No one who crossed our path lacked for food, drink or dessert—on our side of the house or next door with the Eastons.

For almost every evening after dinner, Uncle Carl would knock on the middle wall from his side of our double home. That sound signaled that his pot of coffee was brewed and ready to be served, right alongside his famous homemade banana breadcake. Sometimes joining us for this special blend of food and drink were Aunt Anna, another of my mom's sisters, and her husband, my Uncle Tony Fort.

Saturday night, Aunt Anna would make pop-corn in our old iron pot over the stove, and then, like most of America at the time, we'd all gather around the "TV set" to watch our favorite shows: Lawrence Welk, Jackie Gleason, Mary Tyler Moore, Bob Newhart, Carol Burnett; *The Hollywood Palace*, *Petticoat Junction*, *Mission: Impossible*, and more.

For one very short-time period, circa 1973 to 1974, weekend television was heaven. Friday nights began with *The Brady Bunch*, *The Partridge Family*, *Room 222*, *The Odd Couple*, and the slightly edgier *Love, American Style*. Sunday nights closed the weekend with Walt Disney, *Flipper*, *Voyage to the Bottom of the Sea*, Ed Sullivan, and *Mannix*.

Seriously? What more could anyone want from free entertainment in your living room?

But whatever we watched on any night was usually addressed the next day, when my mom's sisters visited for morning coffee. Television wasn't the only topic of discussion, but the gatherings of good people and stimulating conversation were plentiful. Before every last topic was debated, every last drop of coffee was shared and enjoyed along with some form of Danish, donut, or Coogan. Everyone always kissed and, if need be, made up. There were disagreements, of course, but not a whole lot of divorces. All conversations were served with generous portions of compassion, respect, and understanding. Afterward, everyone moved on to the next adventure in their lives.

And those were just the daily activities.

In the spring and summer, various members from all sides of the family, including my dad's siblings, would host or attend picnics. We'd gather at various homes or locales throughout Rochester, or other Upstate New York communities including Waterport, Honeoye Lake, Canandaigua Lake, or Lake George. When it was a good fiscal year for my father, there were travels to Miami, where one of his brothers lived. For the Easter spring break of 1968, we stayed in Florida for two weeks, which meant my parents somehow managed to have my school vacation extended by seven days. We stayed at the Gold Dust Motel during the first week, and at my uncle's house for the second week.

Throughout the years, we attended family weddings and special occasions such as the "Melfidon Banquet." That particular event was held in honor of those connected with the beatific village of Melfi, Italy, the homeland of my father's family (while my mother's family had hailed from Rome).

After each trip, we made our way back home to Erie Street, where we lived in appreciation. We made sure to thank each other for everything—all the simple treasures we awakened to each morning and cherished each night before we fell asleep.

That's how it was for those of us who lived on Erie Street in a house that provided a solid foundation in all respects. At its essence, the structure of our home was built on a bedrock of unconditional love...especially at Christmas.

During that special time of the year, we'd look forward to sledding down the long and narrow driveway that began high on a driveway/hill of a local business. We'd journey to the local firehouse which every December showcased a massive Nativity scene in its front yard. We'd be sure to visit Downtown Rochester, which housed department stores like McCurdy's and B. Forman Co., both located in Midtown Plaza, one of the first indoor malls in the country.

A magical place, Midtown was home to things like the famed Clock of Nations, and the Monorail that was constructed only at Christmas to encircle the mall. Each December this unique interior plaza transformed into a nostalgic cross between some kind of Winter Wonderland and *The Jetsons*, while Sibley's, another department store located across the way on Main Street, would set up their very own Toyland. This other temporary fantasy world was ruled over with mystical regality by Santa Claus and Mrs. Claus, who distributed gifts like noise-making kazoos, and individually-pressed 45-rpm records.

Then-youngsters like myself were fortunate enough to hear our names on those specially recorded conversations between the Clauses. With each play of my own personal 45, Santa would ask his beloved spouse, "So, whose house will we be visiting this year?"

Mrs. Santa would then reply, "Herbie J's house."

Everyone on Erie Street would hear that all played out more than a few times on our old phonograph stereo during many happy Christmastimes.

One year, I actually *became* Santa Claus in a school play, and in another show that was performed in our Erie Street living room with my cousins Mary Sue and Jimmy B. That same year, my cousin Evie helped me with my Christmas list for the entire family, which numbered close to 40 or more.

The gift selection process would not officially begin until Thanksgiving Day when a "Secret Santa" lottery was held by all the tributary family members at Aunt Anna's house. After dinner, we'd each write our names on a little white piece of paper that would be placed with others in a brown paper bag. From there, we'd "pick names."

Before "Black Friday" got out of hand and expanded into "Cyber Monday," the day after Thanksgiving was designated as the first and biggest sincerely legitimate shopping day of the year.

On many such days, my mom and I would go Christmas shopping with my Aunt Rita and my cousin Jimmy T. at the suburban Greece Town Mall and Long Ridge Mall. The budget for us kids was small, but we made it work. We'd buy things like McDonald's gift certificates for 50 cents each, or sometimes an entire book for $5.00. We'd select doilies and mug trees for the aunts and beer mugs for the uncles. One year, to everyone's amusement, we went to Woolworth's and purchased three "unmentionables" for a dollar, and then gave one to each of the female cousins.

It was a happy, simpler time when no cared about how much was spent on gifts. It wasn't about money. It was about sharing, and just being together. That was enough. Yes, there were challenges, adversities, and grim times. Hurt feelings never lingered too long. No one ever schemed to "out-buy" anyone else. It was a sweet existence in which bitterness always faded into nothingness. For nothing negative ever kept any of us from something positive on Christmas or any other day.

We'd look forward to family meals all the time but especially dinners served on Christmas Eve and Christmas Day, with all the various families attending.

We chose to exchange gifts on Christmas Eve, not Christmas Day. Just one child was selected each year to distribute the presents to everyone else. But before long, all children in the room would soon be handing out packages. Though either way, the lesson was clear and always this:

Love the gift-giver, and not the gift. Or as Mother Teresa once said, "The person who gives with a smile is the best giver because God loves a cheerful giver."

More often than not, such holy and holiday thoughts taught us to ignore our differences and to concentrate on what makes us the same: our humanity.

With that being said, all these decades later, our family, like many in contemporary times, is spread out in different parts of the country and the world. Not everyone can be acquainted in the physical. But it's through the simplicity of something like watching a Christmas TV special or recalling a certain memory that we are re-introduced to one another, or maybe even meet for the first time.

Every December, the gaps close between us all; individuals, families, groups, communities, cities, states, provinces, nations, cultures, and religions. We are kinder to each other. We listen to those who are not heard, speak to those who are ignored and care about those who are disregarded. We reach out to those who are unreachable, play with those who work too hard, and laugh with those who shed too many tears. We make angels in the snow or buy our true love their favorite perfume or cologne. We give to those who sometimes only know how to take and keep, offer peace where there is unrest, and so on and so forth and so good. These are the personal things and intimate moments from which holiday memories spring and just a few examples of the December discernments to behold in this book.

The 12 Best Secrets of Christmas: A Treasure House of December Memories Revealed has been garnered from my youth. But in a way, these memories are from everyone's youth. The chapters are classified as "secrets," with each revealing a special sentiment that may prove recognizable to all. Numbered from one to twelve, the chapters coincide with the mainstream identification of the popular carol, "The 12 Days of Christmas." While that famous chant is referenced in "The 6th Secret" section of this book, *every* chapter offers its own separate insight into the many messages and favorite things that the holiday brings and represents.

Every part of this collection of recollections, if you will, is filled with personal, true, and happy tales that are presented in a straightforward manner. Some of the memories are brief; others are long. But with each page, the message is clear, familiar, and revealing. Once disclosed, the personal, clandestine recollections become familiar to all. The chapters offer joyful recall, acting as hidden trinkets and secret reminders of holiday cheer; time portals to past celebrations for the present and the future. And I hope you enjoy them all, now, and forever.

The First Secret

Think Outside the Box

"**C**ome on, Dad!" I pleaded. "*Rudolph the Red-Nosed Reindeer* is going to be on television next week. We have to put up the red bells that play his theme song and all of the other Christmas decorations too!" From the moment in December 1964 that I noticed the perennial holiday classic advertised in *TV Guide*, that's all my family would hear me say.

Of course, you would also hear my father. "This kid never stops," he would fluster. "He never stops!" He was right. I never did. But I couldn't help it. Each year, I couldn't wait to watch *Rudolph*, narrated by Burl Ives (the Snowman), and other animated musical television specials like *A Charlie Brown Christmas*. Vince Guaraldi's jazzy score from that *Peanuts* classic, and his beloved compositions like, "Christmas Time Is Here," always warm my heart. When Linus recites the Nativity from the Bible to the mainstream American audience, *A Charlie Brown Christmas* becomes more than just a holiday TV special.

Other small-screen December TV favorites include *Santa Claus is Coming to Town* (narrated by Fred Astaire, with

Mickey Rooney heard as Santa), and *Frosty the Snowman* (narrated by Jimmy Durante with Jackie Vernon voicing Frosty). But it was *Rudolph the Red-Nosed Reindeer*, and those red bells, that officially signaled the Christmas season to begin. Rudolph's story of *deer pressure* was universal. As the fable unfolds, his bright snout becomes a dilemma, especially when he develops a crush on a doe named Clarice, who is a comfort, a joy, and a real doll (literally!).

At one point, Rudolph becomes entranced when Clarice sings, "There's always tomorrow…for dreams to come true" (for shiny noses to lose their luster). Along with "Holly Jolly Christmas," and so many other charming tunes from the special, "There's Always Tomorrow" remains unforgettable. It's especially adored because after Clarice finishes singing it, she kisses Rudolph on the cheek and calls him cute. To which he then heralds, "I'm cute! I'm cute! She thinks I'm cute!"

Rudolph then proceeds to fly for the first time (the world-renowned rite of passage for Santa's reindeer); something he was previously incapable of doing. Before he was too self-conscious of his issue. That's why "all the other reindeer used to laugh and call him names." But now, Clarice's love gives him strength, and fortunately, we all get caught in the fallout. She offers hope for every little boy who isn't a picture-perfect school athlete of the year. She demonstrates how every little girl should perceive her sometimes overwhelming Barbie and Ken world. She loves Rudolph for who he is and not what he can do for her. She loves him from the *inside, out,* despite his appearance and outcast status. She's the woman strong and smart enough to stand, with uncommon uprightness, sensitivity, and maturity, behind this boy who is growing into a man.

Strong characters abound in *Rudolph*. There's Hermey, also called "Herbie," which, of course, delighted me, even though his name changes halfway through the show. He's the independent elf with a contemporary view who seeks *elf-improvement* and has little desire to exist as an ordinary imp. Hermey/Herbie wants to be a *denn-tist*. There is the strong-willed, brave, weather-bearing, no-bones-about-it Yukon Cornelius and his fearless band of sleigh dogs. Next, a discerning Santa Claus has the poise to admit when he's wrong, while Burl Ives's kindly, stable, and wise Sam the Snowman explains the North Pole genesis of Christmas trees. "Yep," he says early on, "...this is where we grow 'em."

Who can turn away from the lion King Moonracer? He's the one who rules the Island of Misfit Toys where playthings like little trains with square wheels and water pistols that shoot jelly are discarded. Near the end of the story, the elegant feline royale laments, "A toy is never truly happy unless it is loved by a child," and we believe him. With moments such as these, *Rudolph* glows with style, and like *A Charlie Brown Christmas*, becomes everything a Christmas television special should be – and more.

Many seasons after I first watched *Rudolph* as a child, it was comforting to see students in my college study lounge still watching the show on TV. I thought, *"How cool that I am not the sole 'Rudite' of my generation."* Also, years following *Rudolph's* debut, the advertising firm that represented Norelco's 1960's electric razor TV commercials broadcast during the special—the one with Santa riding a razor on a snow-bound mountain—was inundated with viewer appeals to rerun its original campaign.

At last, even the business world accepted Rudolph. And isn't *acceptance* really what *Rudolph the Red-Nosed Reindeer* is all about? The show's shining star and his band of stop-action animated friends help us to look beyond our differences and to concentrate on what makes us the same. They teach us compassion and tolerance and assist us in comprehending the importance of encouragement (e.g., to give courage) and the destructiveness and outright cruelty of name-calling and mocking. The beloved TV special screams with compassion, "Be who you are and not what everyone tells you to be. All will one day notice your unique traits and the gifts you have to offer the world. Your time will come. Just hang in there. Repeat to yourself, 'I'm cute. I'm cute. I'm cute,' and remember, 'There's always tomorrow.'"

The Second Secret

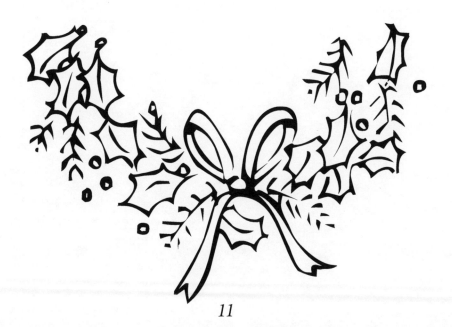

Listen to the Music

I t was always a big deal whenever we got something "new" on Erie Street, whether it was a large appliance like a washing machine or something as seemingly insignificant as a frying pan. Either way, we learned to appreciate everything we had, brand-spanking-new or ancient. To this day, I consider everything I purchase as significant, whether it's a new car or a fresh bar of soap. I never take anything for granted.

That's why what transpired one Christmas, in 1972, became so tremendous an event in my then-little-12-year-old life. That was the year I went with my parents and sister to McCurdy's Department Store in Midtown Plaza. My dad parked his 1969 green Pontiac Catalina in the indoor mall's four-story garage and, the moment we entered McCurdy's main entrance, he turned to the three of us, and said, "Come on...follow me."

In a few moments, we found ourselves in the electronic department at McCurdy's. We were entranced by various TVs and stereos of every make, brand, and style. At one point, Dad stopped suddenly in front of a Magnavox stereo with a turntable and an 8-track player. "So, what do you think?" he asked. "Do you like this one?"

Dad had recently purchased a relatively high-end Hitachi table-top cassette tape player, along with a few new Christmas cassettes by Nat King Cole, and more. All of those added to our old-school collection of holiday LPs by Bing Crosby, Dean Martin, even an original rendition of *Rudolph the Red-Nosed Reindeer*, and others.

When my father now pointed to the big Magnavox stereo in McCurdy's, my mom, sister, and I weren't exactly sure how to respond. At first, we just stood there and exchanged puzzled glances. Then, with a measure of shock, awe, joy, and apprehension, we finally replied to Dad's question with a simple "yes," and a cautious nod. Of course, we liked the Magnavox. How could we not? It was beautiful; a musical component comprised of modern, sleek, oakwood, and black lacquer design.

Upon hearing our eclectic response, my father said, "Good." He then turned to find a store clerk, and purchased the stereo right there, on the spot, in front of our eyes—like magic. We all were so happy, especially me. We all loved music and loved to dance, which we did for years by way of our old phonograph stereo. In addition to our contemporary Hitachi cassette player, we now had a new, modern Magnavox stereo. And one of the first things we heard came from the "easy listening" station on the FM stereo dial; the one where the "red light" denoted that special musical sound.

There is just no way to properly describe what a wonderful Christmas gift the new Magnavox stereo was, particularly because our family was not exactly rolling in cash. But somehow my dad found the extra dollars to buy that new stereo, which I think cost about $199.00.

That was a significant sum for a financially strapped family in 1972, but more importantly, it was a priceless gift.

The Third Secret

Let It Snow

I t was the first snowfall of 1968. "My goodness," Miss Nelson said to those of us in her second-grade class, "You people act as though you have never seen snow before." We, of course, had indeed seen snow before but not for a while. Months of warm, sunny weather had proceeded weeks of fallen, colored leaves, which we had pasted into scrapbooks and called *art*.

I remember sitting in the classic-styled, wooden classroom desks—the kind that were joined together and that we had to dust underneath and around before we left school each day. On this one day, Miss Nelson was at the front of the room holding a science or other type of textbook in her left hand. But to our right and out of nowhere, braided, white flakes descended from the sky.

Most years, the snow arrived before *Rudolph*, and when it did, Miss Nelson was right. My classmates and I did indeed act as though we had never seen snow before. We immediately left our seats and ran to four large windows framed in gumwood, which is rarely used today in any school, let alone any home or place of business. Our "oohs" and "aahs" echoed throughout the room. The snow renewed us. We were recharged. Together, those singular white flakes became something great. Once outside, we played in it, with it, and on it. As with its more solid, cinnamon-colored cousin – the sand on the beach – we even created with it.

Yet with the sand, water is needed to make a kind of clean mud. On the shore, you have to watch for waves. Otherwise, castles topple before any drawbridge can even be designed. But because snow holds water before it touches the ground, it's even better. And as children, we knew that. The flakes kept falling, adding more weight to the happy structure with a carrot for a nose and "two eyes made out of coal," as that *Frosty* favorite Christmas carol goes.

The best things about that snow were the angels it helped us to make and the wings it gave us to fly as if it was our job to somehow, in some way, return the flakes to the sky.

In this way, it was indeed just as Miss Nelson had said.

It *was* her "goodness."

And ours.

The Fourth Secret

Look for the Silver Lining

Christmas of 1972 was the first year we put up a green artificial tree. We had given away our seven-foot silver structure to a neighborhood family who was unable to afford a tree of their own that year. Gone with it were the rainbow, teardrop ornaments that hung upon the tinseled limbs with care. Nowhere to be seen was the fluorescent, circular lamp that colored the bright grey tree as it electronically twirled.

What did return was the silver paper my father would bring home from the Stecher-Traung Lithograph Company, where he worked hard every day for years. No matter what kind of tree we had, that silver paper, with which we also wrapped gifts, would be under it. And the first year of the green artificial tree was not any different. Around the bottom of the tree, over the silver paper, was a red blanket that draped the tree stand. We didn't have a real fireplace, but red-brown-and-white brick-styled paper covered the wall behind the tree.

The impression in our front room was that of a new old-fashioned Christmas. The view from inside the house paled in comparison to the view from the street, where I quite often found myself, the night we set up the green tree. "Go and see what it looks like from the outside," my father requested. It was freezing out there. It looked like the filming location for *Ice Station Zebra*, and he wanted me to check out the special effects.

But no matter. On would go his five-sizes-too-large galoshes over my tiny feet, which tripped each step of the way. I slipped my sister's knee socks over my pants so I would look like Batman, and I was ready to go. Overburdened with clothes, deeds, and heightened imagination, I went out into the cold, blue yonder, looking like that little kid from the Campbell Soup commercials who was smothered in leggings from head to toe.

As I peered earnestly from the sidewalk at our fabricated, if jolly green giant tree, my burdens lightened. The house windows were frosted perfectly around each frame. The tree seemed to smile each time its lights blinked on. Only for a moment did I miss the silver tree. I remembered seeing it in a box in the basement and how compelled I felt to open it each time I had passed it by, be it in December or July.

I finally and fully understood "the silver lining." I knew in my heart about how happy that family must be to whom we gave the silver tree. We had a new tree, and now, so did they.

"Christmas really does grow on trees," I thought as I stood there and shivered.

"Even artificial ones."

The Fifth Secret

Check the Mail

We always enjoyed receiving Christmas cards on Erie Street.

One year, I remember Mom being surprised when she read one from a friend she had not heard from in a long while. "She's such a good person," my mother told me. "She used to hold you when you were a baby. Your eyes would sparkle, and you would dance, right there in her arms."

"Oh, come on, Mom!" I squirmed.

"Yes, you did," she insisted with a hint of good tears. Upon receiving that card, Mom was happy. And that made me think about how special the job is of those who delivered the mail. The work of mail carriers may seem ordinary, but their work is extraordinary. They may not be high-end professional doctors or lawyers, but the printed gifts they bear still fix and defend hearts. They may be the same people who also bring us bills, but at least they don't collect them.

I shivered at the thought, but I also shivered from the frost in the front doorway each time I'd reach in the mailbox for Christmas cards. Yet, too, I felt warm and cozy with enthusiasm for the mail we'd receive every day in December.

I thought about all the people who the mail carriers made happy at Christmastime—all the cards that are delivered each year, especially the ones that arrived just in time—on Christmas Eve.

There were also the special-order cards and envelopes with the embossed family names. Back in the day, those designs were a rare find, sometimes marketed by neighborhood kids as part of some school campaign. Many would knock on our door with their pitch.

"It'll cost about one dollar and twenty-five cents. You get twenty cards with twenty envelopes and your name signed on them. They're really nice and worth the price."

My sweet mom was won-over by the seller's charm and the card's designs. "Okay," she'd say, "...sounds like a good deal. I'll take one order."

Weeks later, the cards arrived with a modest elegance. They paled in comparison to the more expensive designer set, which Mom had purchased for half-price at the drug store during an after-Christmas sale the year before. However, when all the cards were spread out on our kitchen table, ready to be written and stamped, something special happened.

Almond cookies were out in full force, served with milk and coffee. My parents would gather various address books, which showed the wear and tear of many years—usually from being stuffed underneath miles of washcloths in a kitchen drawer. My mother would dampen one of those washcloths, place it on an old salad plate and use it to wet the stamps. As we'd write various Christmas greetings in the cards, the table would be covered by a white and red tablecloth with a poinsettia design. Another tradition was in the making. Be there rain, sleet, sun, or snow, the Christmas cards were signed, sealed, delivered, and received, assuredly, with lots of love.

The Sixth Secret

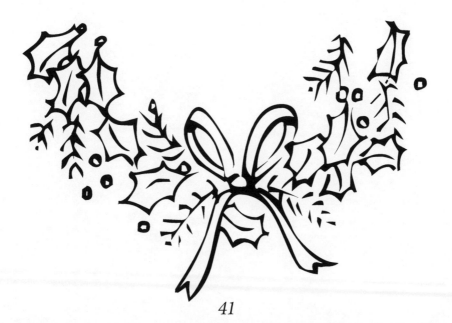

Appreciate the Little Things

I n the Erie Street duplex that we shared with the Eastons, a connecting door on the second level allowed residents from either side to visit each other. I took advantage of this option especially around Christmas because Uncle Carl, Aunt Elva, and Evie on the *other side* knew how to celebrate the holiday. So, I would sneak over to their home whenever I had the chance.

It was the varied aesthetic expertise of Uncle Carl that mesmerized me. A master carpenter and gardener, he one year planted a vine that eventually grew to wrap around the entire house, clinging to each red brick. Every year, he would illuminate the back of the house with all kinds of Christmas lights and decorations that would hug our big back porch. Once the expressway was built on the newly-mounted hill close to our home, the cars driving by would be dazzled by Uncle Carl's blinking lights.

On the interior of the house, Aunt Elva would showcase a particular Christmas prowess of her own. No one opened gifts with as much grace, patience, and appreciation as my cousin Marie, who was the daughter of my mom's brother Joe

Turri. But no one could wrap gifts like Aunt Elva, who did her dandy work on her kitchen table. She would pamper and angle each corner of the gift, making sure that every package was encased perfectly with some formation of ribbon or bow.

Along with the usual assortment of gifts, Aunt Elva one year wrapped a large number of socks and pajamas (a.k.a. *pj's*). When I asked her why, she said, "I don't know, Herbie J. I guess Christmas just doesn't seem like Christmas without a pair of socks and pajamas under the tree."

I thought about that for a moment and agreed. Pj's (especially those designed with the foot warmers) and socks (because of the fireplace custom) fit comfortably with the warm feelings and sugar plum visions associated with Christmas.

When Aunt Elva was finished, I kissed her goodnight, thanked her for letting me watch, and journeyed back to my side of the house. On my way, I noticed a Christmas card on my cousin's desk in the living room that displayed the lyrics to "The 12 Days of Christmas." While happy that I finally got to learn all the words, it was at that same moment I caught my first glimpse of what has become my favorite Christmas decoration of all time.

To explain: some years before, Uncle Carl had constructed something he called a "see-way" in the middle of his living room wall: a built-in wall-unit that you could peer through from one room to the other. At Christmas, the adornment at the center of this unique structure fascinated me. It was a minuscule church with a five-watt bulb that kept it illuminated. Many times, I imagined what it would be like to fit inside those tiny chapel doors and become part of its magic. I remember trying to get as close as possible, gazing, pensively, and being charmed. I never saw anything but a light bulb, but the holy place, that this chapel represented, offered comfort.

On that one of many special Christmases with the Eastons, I learned that good things really do come in small packages. After I peered one final time inside that little church, I climbed the stairs on the way to my side of the house. I turned back to view Aunt Elva as she was wrapping one last gift. With butterflies all aflutter in my tummy, I hoped she was wrapping my box of socks and pajamas.

The Seventh Secret

Shop at All of the Right Places

"Maybe I'll ask your father to take us to Mary's Gift Shop," my mother said one year. "You know where that is, don't you? Near the florist that always has such pretty little decorations in the window."

I knew exactly where it was but had always thought Mary's Gift Shop had been closed because it was so dark and dingy all of the time. It wasn't a very Christmassy place at all.

"Why can't we go to a real Christmas store," I whined, "like McCurdy's or Sibley's or somewhere else downtown?" But my complaints remained unheard. We still ended up at Mary's. My father stayed put in his Pontiac Catalina and kept the engine running. My mom and I walked into the store, thinking that we would not be that long. But we were.

Mary's Gift Shop's door opened with only the slightest ring from the Christmas bell atop its archway. Mary stood behind a smoked-glass counter, which was covered with what seemed to be the largest and most unique assortment of knickknacks and satin dolls in history. A frail, older woman, Mary was both pleasant and sad. It was Christmas, and she was alone in her dismal, little store. There wasn't an employee or customer in sight except for me and my mother.

What does she talk to herself about? I wondered. *Forget downtown*, I begged silently. *Let's just go home!* But I was wasting energy and decided to just browse the store. It did possess a certain coziness, otherwise known as a child's ambiance. It reminded me of when I used to build "forts" with the neighborhood kids. I felt safe and liked it.

I occasionally glanced outside and noticed that the steam from my father's car's muffler was visible due to the cold air. "Hey, how long are you people going to be?" he would lip-synch as he shivered from inside the car. Dad was partly serious, half-kidding, and very cold.

I then heard my mother say, "Oh, aren't those beautiful." She was commenting on a display of high-quality, woven, satin sheets. My aunt and uncle had recently remodeled their bedroom, and the linens would be the perfect gift.

In effect, Mary had completed a sale.

As we began to leave, I noticed Mary smiling, as she waved goodbye. Her gift shop was located near an old black railroad bridge. On many a day walking under that bridge on our way home from school, Pam, Evie, and I had pretended that if we didn't move quickly, the train above us would fall and *destroy* us. "Pam + Mike" (a visual testament to my sister's first love) could be seen in big, white-chalked graffiti, which had been placed there some six years earlier, under one side of the bridge. I thought about how wonderful it was that such a memory has not been erased over time.

However, it was now I who would have a clear, new image that would never disappear. While driving away from Mary's in my dad's Catalina, I peered through the rear window toward her cherished little shop. I recalled how dreary it had looked when we had first approached it. As we drove further away, the less-than-prestigious sign, which had been placed above the quaint emporium, now seemed to glow.

That's when I knew that we had shopped at one of all the right places.

And for once, I was glad that we didn't go downtown.

The Eighth Secret

*Never Lose Your
Sense of Humor*

Every Christmas, my sister Pam, with her excellent taste, would always choose the perfect gift for anyone who was fortunate enough to receive one from her.

One year, Pam purchased an elegant singular tea-cup-and-saucer set for each of my father's sisters. That Christmas morning, with her special packages in hand, along with my parents, and myself in tow, Pam visited the homes of Aunt Alice A., Aunt Sue, and Aunt Fay. I'll never forget the exquisite joy that was delivered that day with each of those delicate gifts.

Other years, back on Erie Street, Pam used to stash several gifts in her bedroom for safekeeping, late delivery, or just because she didn't "want them under the tree right now." At times, her patient philosophy worked in my favor. Since the packages were upstairs and away from the main activity, it was easier for me to pencil in my name after the word *from* on the various name tags. So, of course, I wanted in on the joy-giving, little-brother style.

It was because of these types of maneuvers that my father in his own playful, colloquial way labeled me a "big shot" or my personal favorite, "A real apple knocker." The topper, actually, was hearing my sister scream to our parents, "Did you see what your son just did? So, what are you going to do about it?"

Little did we know that she would be asking these questions for the rest of our lives, with a smile and more laughter as the years go on.

In any case, I buy my own gifts for people now.

The Ninth Secret

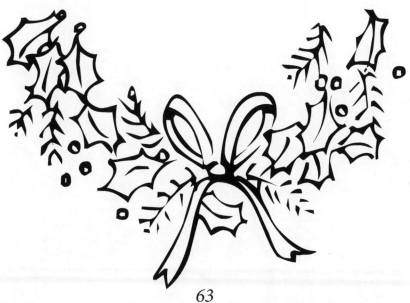

Set a Nice Table

O n many a day, Christmas or otherwise, I would sit on the kitchen floor with both arms parallel to the cupboards, gripping the counter and swinging from side to side. For one reason or another, I'd get that "cozy" feeling again, as I'd investigate the food-filled interior and find Hershey's syrup, Lipton noodle soup packages, paper cupcake molds (a whole box of them), and more.

One December, my mom firmly requested that I get off the floor and help set the table.

"Aw, Mom, do I have to?" I whined.

"Well, what do *you* think?" she replied.

That was the year we hosted a sit-down dinner in our kitchen for approximately thirty relatives. The other rooms were unavailable because there were gifts everywhere: under the tree, by the desk in the living room, near the stereo in the den, and crowded into the dining room. In some parts of the house, colorfully wrapped gifts were piled high to the ceiling.

There was even a gift, a bone, for our dog, Boo Boo, an adorable American Toy Shag. I'll never forget it. Boo ripped that package open with his teeth, prompting Aunt Amelia to tape the bow to his furry, little head. Boo paraded around the house, the life of the party, making everyone laugh at his own delight. "The way he looks at you with those big brown eyes," Aunt Amelia said, "you'd think he was human."

Knowing that good times like these were soon to follow, I was more than happy to set the table, a simple tradition my family had always cherished. On the menu were apple fritters sprinkled with confectionery sugar, assorted meats swimming in homemade sauce (including my mother's faultless meatballs), and other fine foods.

I remember how Aunt Mary had suggested that we use the place settings from my grandmother's special red dinnerware. The cheery, festive red plates set the stage, as I set the table. It was a good idea – one that sealed the silent agreement that each dish served that Christmas was indeed a specialty.

The Tenth Secret

Play Cards

ach Christmas Eve, after dinner, the opening of gifts, and cleaning up, there was time for relaxation. The uncles and older male cousins would play a friendly game of poker. The aunts and those who still wanted to play their own kind of hand would sit around makeshift tables for Liverpool, which was sort of an extended version of Gin Rummy.

As with the dynamic morning coffee hours that my extended family shared almost every day through the year, nerves, and egos clashed galore when playing cards on Christmas Eve. But even more so. Penny-pinching, under-the-breath accusations, sarcastic remarks, and over-winning smiles were present in their full glory or defeat, depending on where you were seated. Outlandish phrases like, "The wrong people are winning!" could be heard clear across the neighborhood.

Yet, there we were, together, every chilly Christmas Eve – with our temperatures on the rise – playing cards and making memories to last a lifetime, and then some.

The Eleventh Secret

Get a Good Night's Sleep

O n one December 23rd, which I used to playfully refer to as "Christmas Adam" (the night before "Christmas Eve"), I went with my parents to visit some of their friends in the suburbs. These *paisons* were a nice stable Italian family: a sweet married young couple who lived in an exquisite home, several luxury cars, and a number of children with their own set of elaborate possessions. They lived well, which was more than evident by the exuberant number of gifts under their very elaborate Christmas tree.

Later that night, when we returned to Erie Street, I was riddled with jealousy. I ran into the living room, looked at our Christmas tree, fell beneath it, and cried. My parents tried to offer comfort and appeasement by surprising me with early gifts they had planned to give me on Christmas morning, which was only two days away. I distinctly remember opening presents like the *Dark Shadows* board game (with vampire fangs, and everything!), and other games like "Hats Off," "Battleship," and "Twister." Although nowhere near the number of packages I had seen just an hour or so before, under the tree at the home of my parents' friends, it was still quite a haul for me to behold.

In the end? Those early presents dried my tears and consoled me for just a short while, only to be replaced by additional tears, this time of embarrassment. I had come to my senses and realized how petty and willful I had been. It was frivolous and ridiculous to assume that children who were more privileged than I would be happier because they had more material gifts and things that this world deems important.

Before that Christmas Adam night was over, a third set of tears would flow, now from an utterly happy heart of awareness. Without a doubt, I knew my most precious gift was life itself, in the simplest measure of the humblest kind. Whatever measure of "true wealth" or "true love" that was and remains within me was placed there by God, funneled through my beautiful mom and dad, as an inheritance from Heaven.

I went on to sleep quite well that Christmas Adam…the following Christmas Eve…the subsequent Christmas Day, and every blessed night forward.

The Twelfth Secret

Make Sure to Shine When You Rise

No matter how many gifts were opened on Christmas Eve, there were always more presents waiting to be unwrapped on Christmas morning. After that, countless assorted foods and desserts were ready to be devoured on Christmas night.

But every year, between Christmas breakfast and Christmas dinner, I always found time to once more visit with the Eastons next-door.

One year, Uncle Carl took his genius carpentry to a new level and created a Christmas threshold of sorts in the Eastons' living room, placing two trees, shining side by side.

Across both sparkling ornamentations, Uncle Carl positioned a wooden arch, which he painted green. In the middle of the arch, he wrote "Merry Christmas," in large white lettering. With some of my father's *magic* silver paper placed beneath the trees, the Eastons' living room looked like their own version of Santa's Toyland at Sibley's department store. With immeasurable joy, I ran up and down the stairwells between our duplex homes. That Christmas morning became one of the most jubilant I experienced on Erie Street. Uplifted in countless ways, I gained a fresh perspective.

Somehow, once again, I had walked through yet another magical Christmas portal at the Eastons' – my second home away from home, which was not that far away from home at all.

Yesterday's Gift is the Present:

An Afterword

By November 1977, it was time to move on – literally. The era of Erie Street was over. I was now 17-years-old, and in my senior year at high-school. Life is about change, and change took place that November.

I moved with my parents and sister to a townhome in Greece, New York, a suburb of Rochester. Aunt Elva and Uncle Carl had also by then left our familiar red brick double house for a new home in Irondequoit, New York, another suburban community nearby. Evie had moved to Los Angeles, and other relatives relocated to different parts of the country, including Phoenix, Arizona. Eventually, everyone in the family—including our beloved dog Boo Boo – was in transition, one way or the other, geographically in this world...or on into the next.

In spring of 1977, I had made my initial visit to Los Angeles, where I would ultimately make the formal move, specifically, to Santa Monica. I would attend U.C.L.A. to study Television and Film, and later serve my internship as a page for NBC-TV in Burbank, California. Before Uncle Carl died, he made Aunt Elva promise that she'd live in L.A. with Evie, "the Doll" (who sadly, passed much too soon at only 62 in 2016). For a few years, I lived in Santa Monica with Aunt Elva and Evie, and her husband of nearly forty years, David Leaf. There, we had our own little "Erie Street of the West."

During the late 1970s, the 1980s, and 1990s, I was blessed with many happy Christmas memories with my parents in their new townhome. I would visit Rochester from L.A. for the holidays, and periodically moved back to Rochester on a temporary basis. Mom, Dad and I would periodically celebrate Christmas Eve with Pam and her husband Sam Mastrosimone and his extended family, and especially their son Sammy, who became more like a little brother to me than a nephew.

By late spring of 2005 – one decade following the death of my father, I was serving as primary caregiver for my mother, who was by then in her late 70s. Even though my sister lived close by, and many good friends had kept a close watch on Mom, I still felt compelled to be in Rochester during this particular time. I knew Mom did not have that many more years left, and indeed, she would pass away in 2008.

But on Christmas Eve of 2005 being in Rochester was more than the right thing to do. By then I was living in a new apartment in Irondequoit, where Mom had eventually relocated as well. Naturally, I wanted to do something special that year for the holiday; something more independent. I lived in a terrific apartment, so I decided to host a Christmas Eve dinner in my own home.

Several lonely souls lived in my apartment building and in the surrounding complex, so I invited many of them over for dinner on Christmas Eve. It was a diverse group that included:

- The fifty-something woman in a wheelchair who lived up the hall. She had married and divorced a multi-millionaire who left her with a hefty financial sum. By the time she had moved into my building, this woman had pilfered away her fortune on poor financial choices. She had also slipped on the ice in the front of her former home and ultimately was left physically disabled.

- The elderly woman who lived two buildings down. She had recently lost her grown daughter to cancer in June of that year.

- The eighty-something male friend of my mom's, whose brother-in-law had raked him for every penny he had, forcing him to live in a senior facility up the block.

- The elderly couple that lived across the hall; he had the early onset of Alzheimer's, and she was too frail to drive across town to spend Christmas Eve with their daughter and her family.

- The dear friend and his mother, whose father and husband had verbally, physically, and financially abused both of them in recent years. They usually spent Christmas Eve alone.

- Another dear friend who had moved to the area from Manhattan. She had just started working at Kodak, had not yet acclimated herself to Rochester, and had no plans for Christmas Eve.

Too many sad stories that needed, if not a happy ending, at least maybe just one happy night, with the potential for a new beginning.

I kept the menu simple. I purchased some frozen ravioli at Wegmans' Supermarket, the Rochester-based, and now-international franchise. As a sauce, I chose the Rochester-based Ragu name-brand and mixed into it some of my own secret ingredients. I bought some green peas, and French bread; added some garlic and butter to both; tossed a salad; and got some wine, soda, and water. For dessert, a few of Wegman's awesome cakes: Lemon, Chocolate, and Apple Cinnamon.

Everyone loved the meal. More than that, they loved the company and the surroundings with a Christmas-card-picture-perfect vision of soft-fallen snow outside. We sang Christmas carols on the inside, and I passed around a few gifts. But nothing elaborate; no diamond watches, cashmere sweaters, or cards filled with cash.

Instead, I had visited the Dollar Store and bought everyone one elegant Christmas ornament. When Christmas

Eve arrived, each guest received one single ornament, and their response was incalculable. You'd think I had given each of them a million bucks. For that one special night, all hearts warmed, and all eyes glistened with tears. Christmas Eve had meant something again…to everyone there. Any and all sadness had melted away, replaced by joyful moments that lingered onto Christmas Day and beyond.

For a few of my guests—the woman in the wheelchair, the woman who lost her daughter, and the elderly male friend of my mom's…it was their last Christmas. Hopefully, it was also one of their best and favorite. I know it was one of mine, certainly reminiscent of all those tremendous years on Erie Street.

And that leads to an illuminating, all-encompassing truth:

It doesn't matter when or where Christmas has been or will be celebrated. Whether it's the 1960s, the 1970s, the 2000s, or today; whether in Upstate New York, Santa Monica, Paris, or Amarillo. More than anything, Christmas is about the company we keep; the delicious meals that are enjoyed, appreciated and shared. As my cousin Mark Borrelli once said, "All food is blessed when it is served with love."

That is to say, every home is blessed on any day whenever and wherever it's filled with any gathering of sweet souls, however they may be defined. Blood relatives, spouses, friends, colleagues, or the like. As long as loving-kindness is a part of the equation, every dwelling is a home, and whoever resides in or visits that home, are family. In this way, every home becomes a home for the holidays.

Christmas reminds each of us—of every good faith and spiritual belief—that there is no time like the present. There are no *presents* like the *gifts* of time we give each other; a treasured state of *now*; a revered state of mind to be experienced in every moment, and at any time of the year.

And that may be the *best...secret* of all.

Acknowledgements

First and foremost, a heartfelt thank you to Dean Butler for writing the Foreword, and to Jerry Houser for writing the Introduction. the honor is all mine to have this book blessed by each of their distinguished contributions.

A very special thank you to the genius of Carole Munshi for her remarkable cover-art for this book, which captures so exquisitely in one image each of the various images I requested.

Thank you, too, to the cover design assistance of Bob Barnett, Dan Holm, and Terry DiOrio; my assistants Wendy Kaiser and Michael Williamson, and the efficient team at Archway, including Sarah Smith, Tim Fitch, Kellie Martin, among others.

For support in a variety of immeasurable ways, thank you to my sister Pamela R. Mastrosimone, my brother-in-law Sam Mastrosimone, my nephew Sammy Mastrosimone; my cousins Marie Burgos, Nicolas Burgos, Joanne Profetta, Jim Tacci, Jim Borrelli, Mary Sue Weigand, David Leaf. Thank you also to Mary Ann Pizzo, and all the members of the

Pizzo, Arioli, Borelli, D'Agostino, Pilato, Piacentini, Sonoga, and Turri families.

Thank you as well to dear friends Robert S. Ray, Joel Eisenberg, Lorie Girsh-Eisenberg, Christopher Pufall, Frank Torchio, Howard Richman, Rudy Anderson, Lex Blaakman, Caryn Richman, Anthony Ferrante, Justin Beahm, Roger Hyman, Sam Amato, Frank Balkin, Andrea Whitcomb-May, Cindy Heiden, Lou Tomassetti, Peter Tomassetti, Edgar Burlington, Keith Anderson, Steve Reeser, Virginia Reeser, Diane Sands, Bruno Salluzzo; Mary McDonough, Thomas Warfield, Vince Staskel, Richard Thomas, Eric Scott, Louis Herthum, Kathy Coleman, Rose Colombo, Richard Michaels, Ed Spielman, Al Schlicher, Barbara Messerle Devitt, Diane Taylor, Jim Smith, Mark Cangiano, Sam and Teresa Montoya, and all my good friends, fellow-parishioners, and clergy at St. Pancratius Church in Lakewood, California.

Thank you also to the countless family members in Heaven including my sweet mother and father, Frances Mary Turri Pilato (St. Frances of Turri), and my father, Herbert Pompeii Pilato (St. Pompeii); Aunt Elva, Uncle Carl, Evie, and Aunt Rita, and countless others. Thank you to all of my relatives, friends, and colleagues, both living and beyond this world; to everyone I know, and love on Earth and in Heaven, and to everyone I have yet to know and love on Earth and in Heaven.

Most of all, thank you God, Jesus, Moses, Buddha, and to each of the Angels and Saints of every good religion and spiritual belief.

Thank you, Everyone.

The 12 Best Secrets of Christmas would have remained a mystery without each of you.

About the Author

erbie J Pilato is a writer, producer, director, singer/songwriter, and entertainment executive who was born and raised in Rochester, New York, across the street from the original home office of the Xerox Corporation, and up the block from the global main office of Eastman Kodak.

Pilato attended elementary school at St. Peter and Paul, St. Augustine and St. Anthony of Padua in Rochester. He graduated high school from Rochester's Aquinas Institute, received a B.A. in Theatre Arts from Nazareth College of Rochester, studied Television and Film at UCLA, and served his Internship as an NBC Page in Burbank, California.

Today a resident of Los Angeles, Pilato has worked for Sony, Warner Bros., NBC/Universal, CNN, Bravo, TLC, E!, A&E, the Reelz Channel, and other film studios and TV networks. In 2010, he founded the Classic TV Preservation Society, a formal 501(c)3 nonprofit organization dedicated to the positive social influence of classic television programming.

Pilato's extensive list of critically acclaimed, media tie-in books include *Retro Active Television: An In-Depth Perspective of Classic TV's Social Circuitry, Mary: The Mary Tyler Moore Story, Twitch Upon a Star: The Bewitched Life and Career of Elizabeth Montgomery, Glamour, Gidgets and the Girl Next Door, Dashing, Daring, and Debonair, The Essential Elizabeth Montgomery, The Bionic Book, NBC & ME: My Life As a Page In a Book, The Kung Fu Book of Caine, The Kung Fu Book of Wisdom, Bewitched Forever,* and more.

Pilato is also a Features Writer for the Television Academy and Emmys.com, the host and an executive producer (with Joel Eisenberg) of his own TV talk show, *Then Again with Herbie J Pilato,* and has recently recorded his second musical CD, *Christmastime with Herbie J Pilato.* More information about Pilato, including a complete list of his books, may be found at www.HerbieJPilato.com.

Printed in the United States
by Baker & Taylor Publisher Services